Love
Around the World

Family and Friendship Across the Globe

WORDS BY ALLI BRYDON
PICTURES BY WAZZA PINK

Acknowledgements

Author: Alli Brydon
Illustrator: Wazza Pink
Publishing Director: Piers Pickard
Publisher: Hanna Otero
Art Director: Ryan Thomann
Commissioning Editor: Nicole Otto
Print Production: Lisa Taylor

Published in December 2020 by Lonely Planet Global Ltd

CRN: 554153 • ISBN: 978 1 78868 493 4
www.lonelyplanetkids.com • © Lonely Planet 2020

Printed in China
2 4 6 8 10 9 7 5 3 1

Stay in touch - lonelyplanet.com/contact

Ireland
Digital Depot, Roe Lane (off Thomas St),
Digital Hub, Dublin 8, D08 TCV4

USA
230 Franklin Road, Building 2B, Franklin, TN 37064
T: 615-988-9713

Love is essential, we need it to live.
Wherever you're from, it is easy to give.

It's yours and it's mine, theirs, hers and his.
Come and see what love is...

In the Netherlands, love is a poem.

On *Sinterklaas* (SIN–ter–class), which the Dutch celebrate in early December, families exchange both gifts and poems.

E ach family member secretly picks the name of the person who will receive their gift and poem. Everyone then purchases a small gift and writes a funny and silly poem about the person who is receiving it, showing how well he or she knows and loves them.

In Japan, *love is a lunchbox.*

Obento (oh–BEN–toe), the Japanese word for lunchbox, is a way for the lunch maker to communicate their love to the lunch eater.

Some Japanese parents rise early just to make the perfect obento for their little ones, and often include fun items they know will make their children smile at lunchtime, such as a rice ball moulded into a popular cartoon character, animals or vehicles made out of colourful vegetables, and *nori* (seaweed) cut into letters.

In Wales,
love is a spoon.

On St Dwynwen's (d'WIN–wens) Day,
January 25th, some sweethearts give each
other beautifully carved wooden 'lovespoons'.

This tradition dates back to the 17th century and is still carried out today. Lovespoons are skilfully carved with symbols: hearts for love, horseshoes for luck and locks for security. The first lovespoons were used for eating, but now they are only decorative and are usually proudly displayed on the wall.

In Iran,
love is a wall.

'Walls of Kindness' are spots where people leave clothing for other people in need. It is said that the first Wall of Kindness appeared in the Iranian city of Mashhad in 2015. Someone painted the wall of a building, put up clothing hooks and wrote in Farsi, "If you don't need it, leave it. If you need it, take it." This is a beautiful way for Iranians to show kindness, charity and love for their fellow citizens.

In China,
love is a lantern.

In the United States, *love is a chocolate.*

On Valentine's Day in the United States, giving chocolate is the way to show love.

Mehndi is beautiful patterns drawn onto a bride's hands, arms and feet using henna, a temporary reddish–brown dye made from plants. These designs adorn the bride as she and the groom declare their love for each other in front of family and friends. This ritual dates back thousands of years and is said to bring good luck to the couple as they start their lives together.

In India,
love is a pattern.

Before some Hindu weddings in India, the bride's female friends and family gather for the *mehndi* (MEN–dee) ceremony.

At the end of Chinese New Year, everyone – from young to old – celebrates the Lantern Festival. This winter's night is illuminated by colourful lanterns, dazzling as far as the eye can see. Music, dancing, laughter and joy fill every Chinese city, town and village. The festival is about family and community togetherness, as the air is filled with light, hope and love. Some call this the 'true Chinese Valentine's Day'.

On February 14th, sweethearts, parents and friends exchange boxes or pieces of chocolate. For many years, chocolate was too expensive for regular people, until English chocolatier Richard Cadbury found a way to make it affordable in the 1800s. Russell Stover, an American chocolatier in the early 1900s, began packaging chocolates in heart-shaped boxes. And that's where the Valentine's Day tradition took off in the United States!

In Kenya,
love is a wrap.

Instead of pushing their babies in prams, Kenyan mothers wrap them in layers of brightly coloured cloth and secure them to their bodies. Mothers carry their babies everywhere: to the market, to pray and even while doing housework. Babies sleep, giggle, coo and see the world from their mother's backs. This 'babywearing', a common practice across Africa, forms close bonds between mothers and children, and surrounds both in comfort and love.

In Mexico,
love is a song.

One way some Mexicans show how much they care is through song, either by serenading those they love or sending a lively mariachi band to perform. Mariachi bands usually have guitars, violins and trumpets, and are arranged to celebrate all sorts of occasions, from birthdays to weddings to Mother's Day. What a musical way to say "¡Te quiero!"

In Fiji,
love is a whale's tooth.

If a man wants to marry in Fiji,
he gives his future father-in-law
a *tabua* (tam-BOO-ah), the
tooth of a sperm whale.

Tabua are sacred, rare and valuable, and a symbol of wealth and position in Fijian society. These whale's teeth can be huge: weighing over a kilogram and the length of an adult's forearm! Since hunting endangered species like sperm whales is illegal in Fiji, tabua are often passed down through families, found on dead whales that wash up on the beach, or sold in second-hand shops.

In Chile,
love is a dance.

The lively, national dance of Chile is the *cueca* (KWAY-ka), most often performed to celebrate Chilean Independence Day on September 18th. But the cueca also features at weddings, funerals, even spontaneously on the street. It is a way to express love, loss, hope and longing. The cueca is danced by two people who circle around while looking into each other's eyes. The dancers wave handkerchiefs in the air and move their feet to the rhythm, never touching. The cueca is said to depict a courtship between a chicken and a cockerel.

In New Zealand, *love is breath.*

For a traditional greeting in New Zealand, two people get close and touch their noses together.

Friends, businesspeople, visitors – many people connect in this way, known as *hongi* (HON–gee). Hongi originally comes from the Māori, the native people of New Zealand. In Māori mythology, the god Tāne–nui–a–Rangi sculpted the first woman, Hine–ahu–one, out of earth. He then pressed his nose to hers and breathed life into her. So, New Zealanders say, to greet others with the hongi is to share the breath of life.

In South Africa,
love is connection.

What could be more loving than to show every human being friendship and respect? In South Africa, the word *ubuntu* (oo–BOON–too) means we are all connected as people.

This 'oneness' brings all the people of the world together as equals. Ubuntu is a reminder of how we should treat others. There are many ways you can model ubuntu: give a smile, say hello, share food and drink, be kind, share toys, help someone in need and recognise that each person is human, the same as you.

Love's a jacket, a meal, a warm hand to hold. . .
A feeling, a family, for young and for old.

Love wraps us up in one ultimate hug. . .

How do YOU show your love?